KEYS TO EXPERIENCING AZUSA FIRE OFFICIAL WORKBOOK

LESSONS FROM THE REVIVAL THAT CHANGED
THE LANDSCAPE OF GLOBAL CHRISTIANITY

JEFF OLIVERR

RICK JOYNER

CONTENTS

Introduction   v
How to use this workbook   ix

1. "Because They Were the Humblest"   1
2. William Joseph Seymour   10
3. The Bonnie Brae Revival   19
4. 312 Azusa Street   28
5. The Deluge   36
6. Parham and Seymour Part Ways   44
7. OPPOSITION AND CRITICS   52
8. THE REVIVAL SPREADS   60
9. THE ANGELS, HEAVENLY CHOIR, BOX, GLORY, AND FLAMES   68
10. Everyday Healings And Notable Miracles   75
11. Brother Seymour   82
12. THE DECLINE, SECOND SHOWER, AND DEMISE   89
13. The Azusa Street Legacy   96
14. The Pilgrims Of Azusa Street   103
15. Beginning Of A Worldwide Revival   110
16. Unlocking Azusa Fire   118

About the Publisher   127

INTRODUCTION

Welcome to the **Keys to Experiencing Azusa Fire Official Workbook**, a journey that promises to not only explore the depths of one of the most significant spiritual awakenings in modern history but also to ignite within you a fresh encounter with the living God. This workbook is crafted to draw you into the heart of the Azusa Street Revival, inviting you to discover the divine keys that unlocked heaven on earth over a century ago. As we delve into these pages together, you will be stepping into a legacy of faith that has the power to transform not just individual lives but entire communities and nations.

The Azusa Street Revival, which erupted in 1906 in a humble mission in Los Angeles, was marked by an extraordinary outpouring of the Holy Spirit. It was a

INTRODUCTION

divine event that transcended race, culture, and denomination, bringing together believers in a unity that reflected the very heart of God. This workbook is designed to bring these historic moments to life for you, offering a pathway to experience the same powerful move of God in your life today.

As you journey through this workbook, you will uncover **ten pivotal keys** from the Azusa Street Revival that are as relevant now as they were then. Each key, from the hunger for God's presence to the unity among believers, leadership guided by humility, and the pursuit of God above all else, will be explored in depth. These keys are not just historical facts; they are spiritual principles that, when applied, can unlock a fresh outpouring of the Holy Spirit in your life and in your community.

Expect to be challenged and inspired as you engage with each section of the workbook. Through reflective questions, actionable steps, words of encouragement, and journaling prompts, you will be invited to not only learn about the Azusa Street Revival but to actively seek a deeper relationship with God. This workbook is not about passive reading; it's about active participation in the journey of faith.

The **reflective questions** are designed to provoke thought and personal examination, helping you to apply

INTRODUCTION

the lessons of Azusa to your own spiritual walk. The **actionable steps** will guide you in practical ways to cultivate an environment in your life where the Holy Spirit can move freely. Words of **encouragement** drawn from Scripture will remind you of God's promises and faithfulness, while the **journaling prompts** will offer you space to record your own experiences, revelations, and prayers as you seek a personal revival.

One of the most profound takeaways from the Azusa Street Revival is the understanding that God is not looking for the equipped; He is looking to equip the called. This workbook is for anyone who desires more of God—regardless of where you are in your spiritual journey. Whether you are a seasoned believer or just beginning to explore your faith, the keys shared in these pages are applicable to you.

As we embark on this journey together, let's approach it with hearts open to what God wants to do in and through us. The Azusa Street Revival was a monumental move of God, but it was just the beginning. The Lord is still moving today, still pouring out His Spirit on all who hunger and thirst for Him. This workbook is an invitation to step into the river of God's presence, to be transformed by His power, and to carry the flame of revival into your world.

INTRODUCTION

Welcome to the **Keys to Experiencing Azusa Fire Official Workbook**. Let's begin this journey with expectation, believing that the best is yet to come, and that through these pages, you will encounter the living God in ways that will forever change your life.

HOW TO USE THIS WORKBOOK

Embarking on a journey with the **Keys to Experiencing Azusa Fire Official Workbook** is more than exploring historical events; it's about igniting a personal revival and walking in the transformative power of the Holy Spirit. To help you get the most out of this workbook, here are ten key points on how to effectively engage with its contents and apply its lessons to your life.

1. Prepare Your Heart

Before diving into the workbook, spend time in prayer, asking God to prepare your heart for what He wants to reveal to you. Approach this journey with openness, humility, and a willingness to be transformed. Expect that God will speak to you through the stories, principles, and lessons of the Azusa Street Revival.

2. Engage Actively With Reflective Questions

Each chapter includes reflective questions designed to provoke thought and personal examination. Don't rush through these. Instead, ponder each question deeply, journal your responses, and be honest with yourself. These questions are tools for self-reflection and spiritual growth.

3. Implement Actionable Steps

Actionable steps are provided to help you apply the lessons learned from the Azusa Street Revival to your own life. Make a concerted effort to implement these steps in your daily walk. Whether it's fostering unity in your community, seeking a deeper prayer life, or stepping out in faith to share the gospel, these actions are practical expressions of your desire for more of God.

4. Create a Regular Schedule

Consistency is key to getting the most out of this workbook. Set aside regular times each week for study and reflection. Whether it's daily, every other day, or weekly, find a rhythm that works for you and stick to it. Consistent engagement will help deepen your understanding and experience of the material.

5. Use the Journaling Prompts

Journaling is a powerful way to process what God is doing in your heart as you go through this workbook. Use the journaling prompts to express your thoughts, feelings, and prayers. Look back on your entries over time to see how God has been speaking to you and leading you through your journey.

6. Study in Community

While personal study is crucial, going through this workbook with others can enrich your experience. Consider forming a study group with friends, family, or church members. Sharing insights, experiences, and prayers can provide support, accountability, and a deeper communal understanding of God's movement.

7. Seek the Holy Spirit

The Azusa Street Revival was marked by a profound outpouring of the Holy Spirit. As you work through this workbook, continually seek the Holy Spirit's presence and guidance in your life. Be open to His leading, and don't be afraid to step out in faith as He directs you.

8. Apply Words of Encouragement

Throughout the workbook, you'll encounter words of encouragement rooted in Scripture. Meditate on these scriptures, memorize them, and apply their truths to your life. Let them be a source of strength, hope, and encouragement as you pursue deeper intimacy with God.

9. Embrace Transformation

Be prepared for God to work transformation in your life as you journey through this workbook. Change may come in unexpected ways—be it in your character, your relationships, or your calling. Embrace what God is doing, and be willing to let go of anything that hinders your spiritual growth.

10. Share Your Journey

As you experience personal revival, share your journey with others. Testify to what God is doing in your life. Your story can inspire faith and encourage others to seek their own encounters with the Holy Spirit.

By following these key points, you will not only gain historical knowledge about the Azusa Street Revival but also experience personal revival and a deeper, more vibrant relationship with God. The **Keys to Experiencing Azusa Fire Official Workbook** is your guide to unlocking a fresh outpouring of the Holy Spirit in your life. May your journey through these pages be marked by profound encounters with God, transformative growth, and an ignited passion for His presence and power in your life.

CHAPTER 1
"BECAUSE THEY WERE THE HUMBLEST"

Let the story of Azusa Street remind you that God delights in using the humble and the willing to accomplish His grand purposes. No matter your background, education, or social status, you are a candidate for God's use.

"**God resists the proud, But gives grace to the humble.**" (James 4:6 NKJV).

In reflecting on the journey that led me to write about the Azusa Street Revival, I'm reminded of the profound impact that **Rick Joyner's Influence** had on my decision. When Rick, a seasoned author and an ardent student of church history, expressed his admiration for my work, it wasn't just a compliment; it was a pivotal moment. He saw potential in a single chapter of my previous work that I hadn't seen myself. His suggestion to expand on the Azusa Street story wasn't merely advice; it was a nudge towards uncovering a deeper narrative within church history. This interaction underscores the importance of mentorship and the unexpected ways in which guidance can shape our paths.

In embarking on this exploration, I was drawn to the power of narrative. The **Importance of Storytelling in Church History** became a guiding principle for my work. Just as Jesus used parables to communicate profound truths, I aimed to connect readers with the Holy Spirit's enduring work through storytelling. This approach wasn't about simplifying history but about making it resonate. By weaving together the stories of individuals and communities, I hoped to present a tapestry of faith that was as engaging as it was enlightening.

The narrative of the **Azusa Street Revival's Significance** stands out as a testament to the transformative power of the Holy Spirit. This revival was not just a historical event; it was a demonstration of unity and spiritual fervor in early 20th century America. It challenged racial and social barriers, bringing together people from diverse backgrounds in a shared experience of the Holy Spirit's presence. The revival's legacy in shaping Pentecostalism and its impact on global Christianity cannot be overstated.

In this context, the story of **Dr. Finis Yoakum and the Pisgah Home Movement** offers a compelling example of how personal transformation can lead to community impact. Dr. Yoakum's journey from healing to founding a movement dedicated to serving the marginalized in Los Angeles illustrates the ripple effect of one man's faith and vision. His story is a reminder of the potential for ministry that extends beyond the walls of the church, touching the lives of the poor and downcast with the love of Christ.

The broader revival scene in Los Angeles provided a fertile ground for what was to come. The **Wider Los Angeles Revival Scene** was marked by a sense of anticipation and spiritual hunger that transcended denominational lines. Various movements and individuals were engaged in fervent prayer, seeking a fresh move of God. This collective yearning set the stage for the Azusa Street Revival, highlighting the interconnectedness of the body of Christ in the pursuit of spiritual renewal.

Central to the story of Azusa Street is the **Humility of the Azusa Street Community**. This revival was not led by the socially or ecclesiastically elite but by those who were often marginalized and overlooked. God's choice to use this humble group as the catalyst for a worldwide revival reinforces the biblical principle that God chooses the weak and foolish things of the world to shame the strong and wise. This aspect of the revival is a powerful reminder that in God's kingdom, humility is a prerequisite for being used mightily by Him.

The theme of humility is woven throughout the revival's narrative, underscoring the **Role of Humility in Revival**. The Azusa Street Revival serves as a case study in how humility before God and one another can create an environment where the Holy Spirit moves freely. This humility was not only a characteristic of the revival's leaders but also of the wider community that gathered on Azusa Street, reflecting a collective posture of openness and surrender to God's will.

Reflecting on the **Impact of Azusa Street**, it's clear that this revival was not just a historical footnote. Its inclusion in lists of significant events by secular media speaks to its profound influence on both Christianity and society at large. The revival's ability to draw attention and spark change across the globe is a testament to the power of the Holy Spirit working through humble vessels.

At the heart of the Azusa Street Revival was a deep sense of contrition and **Repentance**. A.G. Osterberg's reflection that the revival began, lived, and ended with tears encapsulates the deeply spiritual and transformative nature of this move of God. These were tears of repentance, humility, joy, and intercession, marking the revival as a genuine encounter with the divine that changed lives and hearts.

Finally, the **Lasting Legacy of Azusa Street** challenges us to consider how God might use us in our own contexts. The revival began in a humble setting, with individuals who were willing to be used by God, regardless of their societal status. This legacy invites us to approach God with open hearts and hands, ready to be part of His ongoing work in the world, always remembering that it is not our strength, but our humility and willingness that He desires.

Reflective Questions

1. What impact does the encouragement of peers and mentors have on your willingness to take on new challenges?
2. How does storytelling shape your understanding of historical events, particularly those related to faith and spirituality?
3. In what ways does the Azusa Street Revival challenge your perceptions of God's choice of instruments for His work?

4. How does humility play a role in your personal spiritual life, and how can you cultivate it more intentionally?
5. Reflecting on the legacy of the Azusa Street Revival, what does it inspire in you regarding the potential for revival in your community or church?

Actionable Steps

- **Cultivate a Heart of Humility**: Regularly reflect on biblical examples of humility and seek to apply their lessons in your personal and communal life. Consider adopting practices that foster a servant's heart, such as volunteering for behind-the-scenes roles in your community or church.
- **Equip Yourself with Historical Insights**: Engage in deeper study of revivals throughout church history, starting with the Azusa Street Revival. This can broaden your understanding of how God moves in diverse contexts and can inspire faith for what He can do in the present.
- **Engage in Prayer for Revival**: Commit to regular, focused prayer for a fresh outpouring

of the Holy Spirit in your life, church, and community. Consider starting or joining a prayer group dedicated to seeking revival and spiritual awakening.

Journaling Prompt

Reflect on a time when you felt God calling you to step out in faith, perhaps in a way that felt beyond your capacity or contrary to societal expectations. How did you respond? What fears or obstacles did you face, and how did God meet you in that place? Consider how this experience parallels the humility and faith of those involved in the Azusa Street Revival.

"BECAUSE THEY WERE THE HUMBLEST"

… KEYS TO EXPERIENCING AZUSA FIRE OFFICIAL WORKBOOK

CHAPTER 2
WILLIAM JOSEPH SEYMOUR

Remember, "For God has not given us a spirit of fear, but of power and of love and of a sound mind."

"For God has not given us a spirit of fear, but of power and of love and of a sound mind." (2 Timothy 1:7 NKJV)

Reflecting on the life of William Joseph Seymour, I find myself deeply moved by the extraordinary journey of a man born into the aftermath of slavery, who would go on to ignite one of the most significant spiritual awakenings of the twentieth century. His story, from his humble beginnings in Louisiana to becoming the catalyst for the Azusa Street

Revival, speaks volumes about the power of faith, humility, and divine destiny.

Seymour's Humble Beginnings in Centerville, Louisiana, as the son of emancipated slaves, set the stage for a life marked by resilience and faith. The environment of his early years, a world still grappling with the aftermath of slavery and the slow march towards equality, imbued him with a profound understanding of suffering and hope. It was in this context that Seymour developed a resilient spirit, grounded in a deep faith that would later define his ministry. His family's struggle for freedom and dignity in a society that was far from accepting of African Americans played a crucial role in shaping his outlook on life and faith.

Moving north, **The Move North**, Seymour's search for better opportunities reflected the broader African American experience of the Great Migration. Despite the geographical shift, the societal barriers he faced due to his race were a constant reminder of the deep-seated divisions within the country. These experiences, however, instead of hardening his heart, seemed to deepen his compassion and his commitment to a ministry that would transcend racial divides.

His **Spiritual Awakening in Indianapolis** marked a turning point in Seymour's life. It was here that he encountered the Holiness movement, which emphasized a personal, transformative experience of the Holy Spirit. This encounter was pivotal, broadening his theological horizons and instilling in him a hunger for a deeper spiritual life. The blend of Methodist and Holiness teachings he encountered laid the groundwork for his later theological developments, emphasizing the centrality of the Holy Spirit's work in the believer's life.

Influence of Holiness and Healing Movements played a significant role in shaping Seymour's theological outlook. Figures like John Alexander Dowie and Martin Wells Knapp, with their emphasis on divine healing and the imminent return of Christ, introduced Seymour to the radical edge of Christian faith. These influences not only expanded his theological understanding but also infused his ministry with a dynamic power and a vision for what the church could be.

The **Calling to Ministry** that came to Seymour after his battle with smallpox was a moment of divine commissioning. His survival and subsequent call into ministry underscored a theme that would define his work: the power of God to redeem and call forth from the depths of despair. This calling was not just about preaching; it was about embodying the transformative power of the gospel in a world marked by pain and injustice.

Meeting **Charles Parham** and attending the Apostolic Bible Training School were decisive moments in

Seymour's journey. Parham's teachings on the baptism of the Holy Spirit as evidenced by speaking in tongues would become a cornerstone of Seymour's own ministry. This period of learning and growth under Parham's tutelage was a time of both challenge and affirmation, as Seymour grappled with new theological concepts that would eventually shape the Azusa Street Revival.

The Apostolic Bible Training School Experience, despite the racial segregation of the time, became a pivotal chapter in Seymour's story. His humility and determination to learn, even in the face of societal and institutional barriers, exemplify his extraordinary character. Seymour's participation in the school, albeit under restrictive conditions, is a testament to his commitment to theological education and spiritual growth.

The Call to Los Angeles represented a leap of faith, a divine assignment that would place Seymour at the heart of one of the most significant spiritual awakenings of the modern era. This move was not merely a change of location; it was a step into his destiny, a divine orchestration that would see Seymour lead a revival that transcended racial, social, and denominational barriers.

Throughout his journey, **A Vision for a Unified Church** remained a central theme of Seymour's ministry. His life and work challenged the status quo, presenting a radical vision of what the body of Christ could be—a community defined not by race, gender, or social standing, but by the unifying power of the Holy Spirit. This vision, born out of Seymour's own experiences of exclusion and his deep-seated belief in the gospel's reconciling power, would become a hallmark of the Azusa Street Revival.

As we reflect on Seymour's life, we are reminded that the history of the church is often written not by the mighty and powerful but by those who, like Seymour, carry within them a divine spark that ignites movements and changes the world.

Reflective Questions

1. How does Seymour's background of overcoming adversity shape his approach to ministry and his message of hope?
2. In what ways do Seymour's encounters with various Christian movements influence his theological development and understanding of the Holy Spirit?
3. Reflect on the significance of humility and perseverance in Seymour's education and ministry. How can these qualities inform your spiritual journey?

4. Consider the impact of racial and societal barriers on Seymour's ministry opportunities. How does his response to these challenges exemplify faith and determination?
5. What lessons can be learned from Seymour's vision for a unified church in addressing the divisions within contemporary Christianity?

Actionable Steps

- **Cultivate a Heart of Humility:** Reflect on Seymour's humility in seeking spiritual education and openness to new theological perspectives. Practice humility in your interactions and spiritual pursuits, recognizing the value of every person's contribution to the body of Christ.
- **Equip Yourself with a Broad Theological Understanding:** Like Seymour, who learned from diverse Christian traditions, seek to understand and appreciate the wide spectrum of Christian theology. Engage with teachings and practices beyond your own tradition to enrich your spiritual journey.
- **Engage in Reconciliation and Unity Efforts:** Inspired by Seymour's vision for a unified

church, take practical steps towards reconciliation within your community. Participate in or initiate projects that bridge denominational, racial, and social divides, promoting a more inclusive and loving Christian witness.

Journaling Prompt

Reflect on a moment in your life when you felt called to step out in faith, perhaps into an unfamiliar or challenging situation, much like William Joseph Seymour did when he moved to Los Angeles to pastor a small mission. How did you respond to this calling? Were there any fears, doubts, or societal barriers that you had to overcome? Consider the qualities of humility, perseverance, and faith that Seymour demonstrated throughout his journey. How can you apply these qualities in your own life and spiritual journey? Write about the impact of taking this step of faith and how it has shaped your relationship with God and your understanding of His purpose for your life.

KEYS TO EXPERIENCING AZUSA FIRE OFFICIAL WORKBOOK

WILLIAM JOSEPH SEYMOUR

CHAPTER 3
THE BONNIE BRAE REVIVAL

Let us take heart from the story of the Bonnie Brae Revival and William J. Seymour's unyielding faith and dedication. Just as the early disciples waited in the upper room for the promise of the Father, so did Seymour and his companions wait in earnest prayer and expectation. Their persistence was met with an outpouring that changed the world.

"He is a rewarder of those who diligently seek Him" (Hebrews 11:6 NKJV)

Reflecting on the dawn of the Azusa Street Revival, I'm drawn to the extraordinary tapestry of events and divine orchestrations that led to a spiritual awakening which would ripple across the globe. The narrative of this revival is not just a historical account; it's a testament to the power of faith, prayer, and the Holy Spirit's transformative work in the lives of those who earnestly seek Him. As I delve into the nuances of this revival, I hope to bridge the past and present, inviting readers to explore how these timeless truths can be applied in our lives today.

The **Los Angeles' Diverse Roots** played a pivotal role in setting the stage for the Azusa Street Revival. The city's rich tapestry of cultures and backgrounds, including a significant black population among the early settlers, created a unique environment that was ripe for a revival that would transcend racial and ethnic barriers. This diversity was reflective of the kingdom of God and set a precedent for the inclusive nature of the revival, emphasizing that the move of God was for everyone, irrespective of their background.

Amidst the backdrop of **Economic Prosperity and Spiritual Hunger**, Los Angeles in the early 1900s was a city on the brink of transformation. The economic opportunities juxtaposed with a deep spiritual longing among its residents created a fertile ground for a revival. Seymour's decision to stay in Los Angeles, influenced by the spiritual and economic climate, underscored the divine timing and placement for what would unfold. This period reminds us that God often moves in times of both material abundance and spiritual seeking, inviting us to find our true satisfaction in Him.

Seymour's Arrival and Initial Challenges in Los Angeles highlight the resilience and divine guidance that marked his journey. Faced with rejection and being locked out of the mission he was invited to lead, Seymour's unwavering faith and dedication to prayer exemplify the perseverance required to pursue God's call, even in the face of adversity. His experience is a powerful reminder that obstacles and challenges can lead to greater reliance on God and ultimately, to the fulfillment of His purposes.

The **Birth of the Bonnie Brae House Meetings** signifies the humble beginnings from which the Azusa Street Revival would emerge. These intimate gatherings, marked by fervent prayer and communal seeking, grew rapidly, reflecting the collective desire for a deeper encounter with God. The expansion from a small home to a larger gathering space mirrors the way spiritual movements often start with a small spark but can ignite a flame that spreads far and wide.

The Role of Prayer and Fasting in the days leading up to the revival emphasizes the spiritual preparation necessary for a move of God. Seymour's commitment to seeking God through prayer and fasting was a catalyst for the spiritual breakthroughs that followed. This discipline underscores the importance of preparing our hearts and being positioned to receive from God, encouraging us to adopt similar practices in anticipation of His work in our lives.

The Arrival of Lucy Farrow brought a direct connection to the teachings of Charles Parham and the experience of the baptism of the Holy Spirit with evidence of speaking in tongues. Farrow's influence and spiritual authority played a crucial role in leading many at the Bonnie Brae house to experience this baptism, showcasing the importance of godly mentorship and spiritual transmission.

The **Outpouring of the Holy Spirit** at the Bonnie Brae house was a defining moment that demonstrated the power and presence of God moving among His people. This outpouring, characterized by speaking in tongues and dramatic spiritual experiences, marked the beginning of a revival that would challenge and change many preconceived notions about the work of the Holy Spirit.

Jennie Moore's Spiritual Experience, including her miraculous ability to play the piano and sing in tongues, highlights the extraordinary ways the Holy Spirit can empower and gift individuals for the edification of the church. Moore's story serves as a reminder that the Spirit's gifts are not limited by our natural abilities and can manifest in unexpected and powerful ways.

The **Expansion to Azusa Street** was a strategic move that facilitated the growth of the revival. The acquisition of the Azusa Street Mission provided a larger space for gatherings, enabling the revival to reach more people. This move illustrates how physical spaces can become hallowed grounds for spiritual renewal and revival when consecrated for God's purposes.

Lastly, **Seymour's Personal Pentecost** serves as a profound affirmation of his faith and teachings on the baptism of the Holy Spirit. His personal encounter with the Holy Spirit equipped him with the authority and conviction to lead the revival with renewed vigor. It reminds us that personal experiences with the Holy Spirit are not just for our own edification but also equip us to lead and minister to others with authenticity and power.

Reflective Questions

1. How does understanding the diverse historical context of Los Angeles in the early 1900s enrich our appreciation of the Azusa Street Revival's impact?

2. In what ways does Seymour's persistence in the face of rejection and challenges inspire your own spiritual journey?
3. Reflect on the significance of prayer and fasting in preparing for a move of God. How can these disciplines be integrated into your life more intentionally?
4. Consider the transformative role of the Holy Spirit as seen in the lives of Seymour and Jennie Moore. How do you desire the Holy Spirit to work in and through you?
5. What lessons can be learned from the humble beginnings of the Bonnie Brae house meetings for those desiring to see spiritual renewal in their communities?

Actionable Steps

- **Cultivate a Heart of Expectation**: Like Seymour and his followers, cultivate a heart of expectation for God to move in your life and community. Begin by setting aside specific times for prayer and fasting, seeking God's presence and guidance.
- **Equip Yourself with Knowledge**: Deepen your understanding of the Holy Spirit's work

throughout church history and in the Scriptures. Study the book of Acts and other historical revivals to equip yourself with a biblical foundation for expecting and experiencing a move of God.
- **Engage in Community Prayer**: Initiate or join a prayer group that is specifically focused on seeking a fresh outpouring of the Holy Spirit. Encourage each other with testimonies of God's faithfulness and expectations.

Journaling Prompt

Reflect on the transformative power of the Holy Spirit as evidenced by the events at the Bonnie Brae house and Seymour's personal experience of spiritual baptism. Consider your own spiritual journey and the role the Holy Spirit has played in it. Have you experienced moments of deep spiritual renewal or empowerment? If so, describe these experiences and how they have impacted your faith and life. If not, journal about your desires and prayers for such encounters. What steps can you take to cultivate a deeper relationship with the Holy Spirit, following the example of Seymour and his community's dedication to prayer and seeking God's presence?

KEYS TO EXPERIENCING AZUSA FIRE OFFICIAL WORKBOOK

CHAPTER 4
312 AZUSA STREET

Trust in the power of unity and community effort. When we come together, with God at our center, we create spaces where His presence feels closest and His work is most evident. It's in these collective efforts, grounded in humility and a shared vision, that we witness the transformative power of faith.

Hebrews 10:24-25 (NKJV) - "And let us consider one another in order to stir up love and good works, not forsaking the assembling of ourselves together, as is the manner of some, but exhorting one another, and so much the more as you see the Day approaching."

In **Chapter 4**, we dive into the heart of the Azusa Street Revival, starting with the transformation of a rundown warehouse into a place where heaven seemed to touch earth. The **Community Effort** to fix up 312 Azusa Street shows us the power of working together, motivated by a shared dream of a spiritual awakening. Volunteers from all walks of life came together, breaking down barriers to create a space where everyone felt welcome. This wasn't just about fixing up a building; it was about preparing for a divine movement unlike anything seen in modern times.

The first convert at the Azusa Street Mission, a **Roman Catholic worker**, highlights the revival's welcoming nature. This movement wasn't limited to one denomination but was a beacon of hope for anyone seeking deeper spiritual truth, regardless of their religious background. This moment underscores the revival's core message: the kingdom of God is open to all, cutting across traditional religious lines.

When we think about the **Improvised Fruit Crates** used for seating and the sawdust on the floor, we're reminded that God's presence doesn't need grandeur. The Lord meets us in our simplicity and earnestness, turning ordinary places into sacred spaces.

The **Spirit-Led Gatherings** at Azusa Street were

different from the well-planned church services many are used to. Here, the Holy Spirit directed everything, guiding each testimony, song, and message. This dependence on the Spirit's guidance created an environment where miracles became common, and hearts were forever changed.

Diverse Participation was a key feature of the Azusa Street Revival, showing the multifaceted family of God's kingdom. The mix of people from different races, social backgrounds, and economic situations in worship and fellowship was a powerful testament to the Holy Spirit's unifying power. This diversity wasn't just a side note but a crucial aspect of the revival's identity and impact.

The **Manifestations of the Spirit**, such as speaking in tongues and healings, confirmed the immediate and powerful presence of God. These supernatural events were not only signs of divine favor but also invitations for all to dive deeper into faith's mysteries. They acted as a tangible link to the experiences of the early church, connecting across centuries and cultures.

Global Attention towards the revival increased as word spread of the extraordinary events at Azusa Street. This international interest highlights the universal desire for genuine spiritual experiences and the power of testimony to ignite faith around the world.

The revival's timing with the **Impact of Natural**

Disasters, like the San Francisco earthquake, offered a poignant context for the spiritual awakening in Los Angeles. These events prompted a greater openness to spiritual truths and emphasized the revival's message of hope amid turmoil.

Considering the **Enduring Legacy of Azusa Street**, we see that the revival's influence goes far beyond its time and place. It inspires us to seek unity, embrace simplicity, and follow the Holy Spirit's lead in our gatherings.

As we delve into the **Transformation of 312 Azusa Street**, let's be motivated by the story of a seemingly insignificant place becoming the epicenter of a movement that would touch millions. This chapter invites us to look beyond appearances and recognize the potential for divine encounters in our lives, encouraging us to ready our hearts for God's transformative work.

Reflective Questions

1. How does the transformation of a physical space reflect the potential for personal and communal spiritual transformation?
2. In what ways can the unity and diversity experienced at Azusa Street serve as a model

for contemporary churches and spiritual communities?
3. How do you see the role of spontaneous and Spirit-led worship in your own spiritual life or community?
4. What lessons can be learned from the humble beginnings and simplicity of the Azusa Street Revival for modern-day ministries and church growth?
5. Considering the global impact of the Azusa Street Revival, how can individuals today contribute to a new spiritual awakening or revival within their own contexts?

Actionable Steps

- **Cultivate a Heart for Unity:** Engage in intentional relationships and community-building efforts that cross cultural, denominational, and socioeconomic lines, mirroring the unity of Azusa Street.
- **Equip Yourself for Spirit-led Ministry:** Dedicate time for personal prayer and study of the Scriptures related to the Holy Spirit's work, seeking to be more open and responsive

to the Spirit's leading in your life and ministry.

- **Engage in Intercessory Prayer for Revival**: Commit to regularly praying for a fresh outpouring of the Holy Spirit in your community, nation, and the world, following the example of persistent prayer that characterized the early days of Azusa Street.

Journaling Prompt

Reflect on the humble beginnings of the Azusa Street Revival and the transformation of its physical space into a hub of spiritual awakening. Consider the spaces (physical or communal) in your life that seem humble, overlooked, or in need of transformation. How can you invite the Holy Spirit into these areas? Journal about how God might use what appears insignificant or inadequate in your life for His glory and for the spiritual enrichment of others around you.

312 AZUSA STREET

CHAPTER 5
THE DELUGE

In the midst of overwhelming growth and the myriad of languages and backgrounds converging at Azusa Street, a reminder stands clear for us today: God's Spirit transcends all boundaries. The incredible unity and diversity at Azusa teach us that when the Holy Spirit moves, He does so in a way that unites us across all conceivable divides. This unity in diversity reflects the kingdom of heaven more accurately than any human institution could.

"Where there is no vision, the people perish: but he that keepeth the law, happy is he." - Proverbs 29:18 (NKJV)

Imagine stepping into a scene where the air is thick with anticipation and the very ground seems to pulse with spiritual energy. This was Azusa Street in 1906, a place where heaven brushed the earth, and the Holy Spirit moved with a **power that defied explanation**. As the author of this journey, I want to invite you into this pivotal moment in history, not as a distant observer, but as a participant feeling every vibration of this spiritual awakening.

By the summer of that year, the tiny warehouse on Azusa Street could barely contain the crowds that flocked to it. Picture over a thousand people, from every corner of society, **gathered in a unity that transcended every human-made division**. It was a melting pot of cultures, classes, and colors, united by a hunger for the divine. The scene was one of chaos to the outsider, but to those within, it was a beautiful harmony of souls in search of God.

This revival was not just a local event; it was a magnet for those **traveling from afar**, drawn by stories of miracles and wonders. Imagine the commitment of these pilgrims, some journeying thousands of miles, driven by a deep yearning to experience God's power firsthand. Their arrival turned Azusa Street into a global crossroads, a beacon of hope and spiritual renewal.

As remarkable as the gatherings were the **miraculous manifestations** that occurred. The divine language of the Holy Spirit broke through, enabling people to speak in tongues they'd never learned. This phenomenon wasn't just for show; it was a sign of the Spirit's presence, a tangible connection to the divine that transcended human understanding.

Amid this outpouring of the Spirit, the **upper room** of the Azusa Street Mission became a sacred space for those seeking a deeper encounter with God. It was here that many were baptized in the Holy Spirit, emerging with new languages and a renewed sense of purpose. This space was a modern-day upper room, echoing the Pentecostal outpouring of the early church.

However, this revival was not without its challenges. As the news spread, **counterfeit spirits** sought to sow confusion and doubt among the faithful. Yet, the community at Azusa Street remained vigilant, leaning on discernment and prayer to navigate these trials. It was a reminder that even in the midst of a mighty move of God, discernment is crucial.

The meetings at Azusa Street were marked by **spontaneous conversions**, moments of divine intervention where hearts were transformed in an instant. These were not conversions born out of obligation but out of genuine encounters with the Holy Spirit. Each conversion was a testament to the revival's power to change lives.

What set Azusa Street apart was its role as a **cultural and spiritual exchange.** It wasn't just about the miracles or the speaking in tongues; it was about the coming together of diverse peoples, each contributing their voices to a chorus of faith that resonated beyond the walls of the mission.

Today, as we reflect on the legacy of Azusa Street, we're reminded of the importance of **cultivating spaces where the Holy Spirit can move freely.** It's a call to foster unity, to seek out the Spirit's presence with expectation and openness, and to participate in the ongoing story of God's work in our world.

In recounting the story of Azusa Street, my aim has been to bridge the gap between past and present, to show how a moment in history can illuminate our path forward. It's a narrative that invites us not just to look back in wonder but to look forward with hope, knowing that the same Spirit that moved so powerfully then is still at work today, inviting us into a deeper relationship with the divine.

Reflective Questions

1. How does the unity in diversity witnessed at Azusa Street challenge your current understanding of community and church?
2. Reflect on a time when you experienced or witnessed the Holy Spirit's transformative power. How did it change your perspective on God's ability to work through diverse groups of people?
3. The revival saw people from various backgrounds speaking in languages they did not know. How does this affirm or challenge your views on the gifts of the Spirit, especially speaking in tongues?
4. Consider the role of prayer and openness to the Holy Spirit in the revival. How can you cultivate a similar environment in your own spiritual community or church?
5. The Azusa Street Revival had a global impact, drawing people from around the world. How can this historical event inspire current and future generations to pursue a deeper, more inclusive walk with God?

Actionable Steps

- **Cultivate a Heart for Unity:** Begin by praying for a heart that sees beyond racial, cultural, and denominational lines, seeking to understand and embrace the diverse ways in which God moves among His people.
- **Equip Yourself with Knowledge:** Study the Scriptures and historical accounts of revivals, like Azusa Street, to understand the importance of unity, diversity, and the power of the Holy Spirit in the body of Christ.
- **Engage in Cross-Cultural Fellowship:** Actively seek opportunities to worship and serve with believers from different backgrounds. Let these experiences broaden your understanding of the kingdom of God.

Journaling Prompt

REFLECT on the unity in diversity experienced at the Azusa Street Revival. Consider the barriers that exist within your own community or church. Journal about how you can be an agent of unity in the Spirit, promoting a culture of inclusiveness and love that mirrors the atmosphere of Azusa Street.

THE DELUGE

CHAPTER 6
PARHAM AND SEYMOUR PART WAYS

In the midst of divisions and challenges, let us remember that God's work is not limited by human disagreements or misunderstandings. The story of Parham and Seymour, despite their parting ways, reminds us that God's purposes prevail. As we seek to lead or participate in spiritual movements, let us do so with humility, love, and a deep reliance on the Holy Spirit.

"Let nothing be done through selfish ambition or conceit, but in lowliness of mind let each esteem others better than himself." - Philippians 2:3 (NKJV)

In Chapter 6, we delve into a defining moment in the Azusa Street Revival, a time when two pivotal leaders in the Pentecostal movement, **Parham and Seymour, found their paths diverging**. This chapter not only captures a significant shift but also brings to light the complexities of leadership and the essence of discernment in spiritual movements. As I share this journey with you, my intention is to draw you closer to the heart of a revival that reshaped the course of Christian spirituality.

Seymour's plea for Parham's guidance in Los Angeles underscores a deep yearning for unity and clarity amidst the burgeoning revival. Seymour, facing the influx of spiritualists and the challenge of discerning the genuine from the false, reaches out to Parham, his spiritual father. This act of reaching out highlights the importance of spiritual mentorship and the reliance on discernment in leadership.

Meanwhile, **Parham's focus on the strife in Zion** reveals the difficult decisions leaders must make when confronted with multiple crises. His choice to prioritize Zion over Los Angeles reflects the complexity of responding to God's call amid competing demands, a scenario that tests the wisdom and priorities of spiritual leaders.

As the narrative unfolds, we see the **expansion of both leaders' movements**, a testament to the hunger for spiritual awakening across communities. This growth speaks volumes about the impact of the Pentecostal message and the universal yearning for a deeper connection with the divine.

Upon arriving in Los Angeles, **Parham's disillusionment with the Azusa Street Revival** brings to the forefront the challenges of balancing doctrinal purity with the raw emotional expressions of faith. His criticisms, particularly regarding the interracial nature of the meetings, shed light on the cultural and doctrinal tensions that can arise within spiritual movements.

Parham's attempt to establish his own meetings in Los Angeles, after being marginalized at Azusa Street, illustrates the struggle that occurs when different visions and leadership styles collide. This episode reveals the resilience of the Azusa Street Revival and the challenges that come with trying to steer a spiritual movement in a different direction.

The role of **Zion in the broader Pentecostal movement**, enhanced by Parham's efforts, underscores the interconnectedness and mutual influence of various Christian traditions on the development of Pentecostalism. This blend of divine healing and Pentecostal spirituality marks a significant milestone in the movement's history.

Parham's later years, marked by accusations and scandal, highlight the vulnerabilities and personal trials faced by leaders of spiritual movements. These challenges underscore the cost of pioneering new spiritual frontiers and the impact of public scrutiny on personal and ministerial integrity.

Lastly, the **contrasting leadership styles of Parham and Seymour**—especially their handling of the revival's challenges—offer a deeper understanding of spiritual leadership. Seymour's decision to remain positive about Parham, despite their separation, emphasizes the significance of humility and unity in advancing God's kingdom.

Through these pivotal moments, Chapter 6 offers a nuanced exploration of leadership, mentorship, and the enduring legacy of the Azusa Street Revival. It's a reminder of the delicate balance between spiritual guidance, personal conviction, and the overarching purpose of spreading the Gospel in an ever-changing world.

Reflective Questions

1. Reflect on the importance of discernment in leadership, especially in spiritual movements. How can leaders effectively distinguish

between genuine and counterfeit manifestations of the Holy Spirit?
2. Consider the role of racial integration in the Azusa Street Revival. What does this teach us about the kingdom of God and the church's call to unity?
3. How do the challenges faced by Parham and Seymour inform your understanding of the costs and complexities of pioneering a spiritual revival?
4. In what ways can the legacy of figures like Dowie and the influence of Zion City inspire current Christian leaders and movements?
5. Reflect on the impact of leadership styles on the direction and health of a spiritual movement. How can leaders maintain a balance between openness to the Spirit and doctrinal integrity?

Actionable Steps

- **Cultivate Discernment**: Engage in regular prayer and study of the Scriptures to enhance your ability to discern between true and false spiritual manifestations.

- **Equip for Unity:** Educate yourself and your community on the history and values of racial integration within the Pentecostal movement to foster a more inclusive and united church environment.
- **Engage with Humility:** Practice humility in leadership, recognizing that the success of a spiritual movement is ultimately dependent on the guidance of the Holy Spirit, not human effort or charisma.

Journaling Prompt

Reflect on a time when you encountered a situation that required discernment between true and false manifestations of spirituality. What did you learn from that experience about the role.

PARHAM AND SEYMOUR PART WAYS

CHAPTER 7
OPPOSITION AND CRITICS

In the face of opposition, remember that perseverance and faith are key. Though we may encounter resistance and criticism, our steadfastness in belief and practice will demonstrate the strength and authenticity of our convictions.

"For God has not given us a spirit of fear, but of power and of love and of a sound mind." - 2 Timothy 1:7, NKJV

As we journey through Chapter 7, "Opposition and Critics," we delve into the complexities and challenges faced by the Azusa Street Revival. It's a tale of passion, division, and ultimately, transformation. From the moment the revival began, it stirred a myriad of reactions across Los Angeles and beyond. Its **unconventional nature** attracted not just seekers of spiritual truth but also significant scrutiny and opposition from established religious groups and societal figures. The revival's **intense gatherings and diverse congregation** broke many social and racial barriers, which was both its strength and a source of controversy.

The **criticisms from established churches** highlighted a common theme in religious history: new movements often face resistance from the status quo. This resistance was not just vocal but took on **practical challenges**, including complaints to law enforcement and health departments, aiming to disrupt or shut down the revival meetings. Amidst these external pressures, internal strife also emerged, leading to notable departures and **divisions within the religious community**. Prominent figures, who initially supported the revival, later distanced themselves or became vocal critics, further complicating the narrative around Azusa Street.

Media coverage played a significant role in shaping public perception of the revival. Newspapers and reporters often **sensationalized the events**, focusing on the most outlandish aspects of the gatherings. This coverage not only influenced public opinion but also exacerbated tensions between the revival and the wider community. Despite these challenges, some critics who came to scoff remained to pray. Their stories of **transformation and newfound faith** underscore the profound impact of the revival's spiritual fervor.

Leaders from various denominations, including those who had been supportive, found themselves **caught in the crossfire of public opinion and doctrinal purity**. They had to navigate the delicate balance between supporting a genuine move of God and adhering to their established beliefs and practices. This dilemma often led to painful separations and the formation of new congregations and movements.

Skepticism wasn't limited to religious figures; it also came from the medical and academic communities. However, the personal testimonies of those who experienced profound spiritual awakenings served as a powerful counter-narrative to the doubts and criticisms. The **enduring legacy** of the Azusa Street Revival, despite the intense opposition it faced, is a testament to its authenticity and transformative power. It's a story of how faith, perseverance, and the Holy Spirit's work can overcome skepticism, division, and hostility.

Reflecting on this chapter, we're reminded of the resilience required to sustain a spiritual movement in the face of opposition. The Azusa Street Revival's journey through skepticism, criticism, and societal pressures is a profound lesson in the power of faith and unity. It teaches us that true spiritual movements often rise above human challenges and become beacons of hope and transformation for many. This chapter encourages us to look beyond the criticisms and divisions, focusing instead on the core message of unity and spiritual renewal that defines such movements.

Reflective Questions

1. How does opposition serve as a catalyst for spiritual growth? Reflect on instances where facing resistance strengthened your faith.
2. What role does inclusivity play in fostering a strong spiritual community? Consider the impact of the revival's stance on racial and social inclusivity.
3. How can we discern genuine spiritual movements amidst criticism? Explore the importance of personal experience and scriptural alignment in understanding the authenticity of spiritual practices.
4. What strategies can be employed to navigate external criticism constructively? Reflect on

ways to maintain faith and unity within a community despite external pressures.
5. How can personal testimonies of transformation influence public perception of a spiritual movement? Discuss the power of personal stories in overcoming skepticism.

Actionable Steps

- **Cultivate** an environment of open dialogue and understanding within your community to strengthen bonds and support each other through times of opposition.
- **Equip** yourself and others with knowledge of scriptural truths and personal testimonies to effectively address criticism and misconceptions about your faith.
- **Engage** with critics and skeptics respectfully, using such interactions as opportunities to share your faith and the transformative power of the Holy Spirit.

Journaling Prompt

Reflect on a time when you faced opposition or criticism for your beliefs. How did you respond, and what did you learn from the experience? Consider how the principles of perseverance, faith, and love can guide you in future encounters with resistance.

OPPOSITION AND CRITICS

CHAPTER 8
THE REVIVAL SPREADS

Trust in the power of the Holy Spirit to move beyond human boundaries and to ignite hearts across the world with God's love and power.

Acts 1:8 - "But you shall receive power when the Holy Spirit has come upon you; and you shall be witnesses to Me in Jerusalem, and in all Judea and Samaria, and to the end of the earth."

In Chapter 8, titled "The Revival Spreads," I want to take you through how the spark ignited at Azusa Street began to set hearts ablaze far beyond our initial gathering place. This spreading of the Holy Spirit's fire was not a planned campaign but rather a spontaneous overflow of believers' hearts transformed by God's love.

The spreading of the revival was something to behold. It felt like watching ripples spread across a pond after a stone is thrown. People touched by the Spirit felt an unstoppable urge to share this experience. This led to the creation of new missions and the spreading of Pentecost's message through various means, reaching out and touching many lives.

Street evangelism became a bold declaration of our faith. Despite facing arrests and harsh opposition, the determination of our evangelists often led to moments where God's power couldn't be ignored. These divine encounters showcased God standing with us, turning our trials into platforms for His glory to shine through.

The **use of Los Angeles' trolley system** turned out to be a surprising but key factor in spreading the revival. These streetcars became our moving stages, taking the good news into every corner of the city. It showed us how God can use even the ordinary parts of our lives to fulfill extraordinary purposes.

Our gatherings were a beautiful tapestry of **racial diversity** that resembled Heaven's congregation more than any place of worship at that time. This diversity was a powerful witness to the Spirit's unifying power, overcoming worldly divisions and creating a community that truly reflected God's kingdom.

Ecumenical outreach fostered a sense of unity and collaboration among various missions and churches, which was vital for the growth of the revival. Regular meetings at Azusa Street encouraged a spirit of mutual support and shared vision among leaders from different backgrounds, highlighting our common goal of seeing God's kingdom on Earth.

Key figures such as Florence Crawford and Glenn Cook played crucial roles in organizing efforts to extend the revival's reach both locally and nationwide. Their dedication and leadership were instrumental in spreading the Pentecostal message far and wide, showing how God equips leaders to guide the movement of His Spirit.

The hard work of our **staff and volunteers**, who managed communications and organized gatherings, ensured that the message of Azusa Street reached a broader audience. This behind-the-scenes effort was essential in connecting and supporting the growing community of believers.

The **national and international expansion of the revival** illustrated the global impact of what started in a humble mission on Azusa Street. Missionaries took the revival's flame to new territories, sparking movements across the U.S. and beyond, echoing the Great Commission in a modern-day Pentecost.

This chapter of our journey shows the vast influence of the revival, not just within Azusa Street's walls but as a catalyst for a global Pentecostal movement. The seeds sown in those who encountered God's power at Azusa Street have blossomed into an extensive, worldwide community of believers, united by the transformative experience of the Holy Spirit.

Reflective Questions

1. How can we, as modern believers, draw inspiration from the spread of the Azusa Street Revival to impact our communities today?
2. What role does prayer and openness to the Holy Spirit play in preparing for a revival in our time?
3. How can we cultivate racial and cultural diversity in our congregations to reflect the kingdom of Heaven on earth?
4. In what ways can we use modern technology and transportation to spread the gospel,

similar to the use of trolleys during the Azusa Street Revival?
5. How important is ecumenical outreach and unity among different Christian denominations in spreading the revival fire today?

Actionable Steps

- **Cultivate** a heart for revival by praying daily for the Holy Spirit to move in your life, in your church, and in your community, similar to the earnest prayers of the early revivalists.
- **Equip** yourself and others by studying the history of revivals, including the Azusa Street Revival, to understand the dynamics of spiritual awakening and the power of the Holy Spirit.
- **Engage** in street evangelism, community service, and inter-denominational gatherings to spread the gospel and the love of Christ, mirroring the actions of those involved in the early days of the revival.

Journaling Prompt:

Reflect on the impact of the Azusa Street Revival's. Consider how a similar movement of the Holy Spirit could transform your community today. Write about the steps you can personally take to foster an environment where such a revival could flourish.

THE REVIVAL SPREADS

KEYS TO EXPERIENCING AZUSA FIRE OFFICIAL WORKBOOK

CHAPTER 9
THE ANGELS, HEAVENLY CHOIR, BOX, GLORY, AND FLAMES

Let us embrace humility and unity, allowing God's Spirit to lead our worship and our lives, just as He did at Azusa Street. In doing so, we become vessels of His love and grace, drawing others closer to Him.

> **"Behold, how good and how pleasant it is for brethren to dwell together in unity!" Psalm 133:1 NKJV**

Looking back on the journey of the Azusa Street Revival, it's like we were part of something straight out of the Bible. Our gatherings were like stepping into a different world, where every song and hymn was a bridge to something divine. We were drawn into deeper conversations with God, not through carefully planned services, but by the spontaneous movement of the Holy Spirit.

Frank Bartleman, a keen observer and participant, felt strongly that worship should be led by the Spirit, not by any person's plan. This way of worship brought us closer to the heart of God and allowed us to experience His presence in extraordinary ways, including **seeing and hearing angels**. Imagine that — angels among us, confirming we were part of something truly heavenly.

The **heavenly choir** was something you had to hear to believe. Picture a group of us, all different, singing in languages we didn't know, in harmony so perfect it felt like angels had joined us. This wasn't just singing; it was an outpouring of our hearts to God, united in a way that words can't fully capture.

When we brought in a **piano** and, for a short time, a **violin**, our worship gained new layers. But even with these additions, the focus stayed on letting the Spirit guide our music, ensuring that every note was a direct response to God's stirring in our souls.

Prayer was our foundation, our starting and ending point. William Seymour, with a humility that spoke volumes, would often pray with a shoe crate over his head. These moments weren't just about asking God for things; they were powerful times of seeking God's presence and inviting His **Shekinah Glory** into our midst.

This holy mist wasn't just something to see; it was God's presence that we could feel and breathe in.

Prophecy played a huge role in guiding us and strengthening our faith. It wasn't just for one person's benefit but for all of us, helping us feel connected to God's plan in a real and tangible way.

Perhaps one of the most stunning signs of God's presence were the **rooftop flames** that people outside the mission reported seeing. Firefighters would come, expecting to battle a blaze, only to find no physical fire, just a supernatural sign of God's power.

At Azusa Street, it didn't matter where you came from, what color your skin was, or how much money you had. We were all seeking God together, and that pursuit broke down walls and brought us together in ways we never imagined. This unity in diversity showed a glimpse of God's kingdom, where everyone is equal in Christ's love.

The **heavenly choir**, **Shekinah Glory**, and powerful times of **prayer** were not just experiences to marvel at but invitations to dive deeper into God's love. The **prophecies**, **angels**, and even the sacredness of **"the box"** were all ways God spoke to us, reminding us of His presence and care.

Reflecting on all this, it's clear the Azusa Street Revival wasn't just an event in history. It was a taste of what God desires for His church: a community united in His love, living out the truth in the Spirit, and showing His glory to the world. As we move forward, let's carry the lessons and spirit of Azusa in our hearts, always seeking to live in the presence of God and in unity with each other.

Reflective Questions

1. How does the idea of a "heavenly choir" influence your understanding of worship?
2. What role do you believe angels play in our gatherings today, and how does this shape your expectations of God's presence?
3. In what ways can you incorporate the principle of humility, as demonstrated by Seymour's use of the box, into your personal prayer life?
4. How does the manifestation of the Shekinah Glory at Azusa Street encourage you to seek God's presence in your community?
5. What lessons can we learn from the unity and diversity of the Azusa Street Revival to apply in our churches today?

Actionable Steps

- **Cultivate** a heart of worship that seeks to be led by the Holy Spirit, embracing both traditional hymns and spontaneous expressions of praise.
- **Equip** your community with the knowledge of Azusa Street's legacy, encouraging them to pursue a deep and authentic relationship with God.
- **Engage** in acts of humility and service, reflecting the spirit of unity and love that was evident at Azusa Street, breaking down barriers within your own context.

Journaling Prompt

Reflect on the concept of the "heavenly choir" and the role of the Holy Spirit in guiding worship. Consider how you can contribute to a worship experience that invites the presence of God, just as it was at Azusa Street. Write about ways you might foster unity and humility in your spiritual community, drawing inspiration from the diverse and Spirit-led gatherings of the revival.

KEYS TO EXPERIENCING AZUSA FIRE OFFICIAL WORKBOOK

THE ANGELS, HEAVENLY CHOIR, BOX, GLORY, AND FLAMES

CHAPTER 10
EVERYDAY HEALINGS AND NOTABLE MIRACLES

Let's remember, in the midst of our daily struggles and when facing seemingly insurmountable obstacles, that we serve a God of miracles. The same power that flowed through the Azusa Street Revival, bringing healing and transformation to countless lives, is available to us today. Encouragement is found not just in the miraculous but in the promise that God is with us, in every trial and every moment of need.

"By His stripes we are healed." - Isaiah 53:5 NKJV

In Chapter 10, titled "Everyday Healings and Notable Miracles," we explore a series of extraordinary events that unfolded during the Azusa Street Revival, demonstrating the power of faith and prayer in action. The chapter begins with **The Upper Room as a Place of Miracles**, a sacred space where countless individuals sought and found healing. Here, through faith and persistent prayer, the sick were made whole, illustrating the revival's profound spiritual impact.

The narratives of Emma Cotton and Florence Crawford are particularly moving, showcasing **Everyday Faith in Action.** Their stories of miraculous healing remind us that faith isn't just for the extraordinary moments but for our daily lives, offering hope and transformation.

A striking aspect of the revival was the active involvement of young believers, highlighted in **The Role of the Youth**. Young people weren't sideline spectators; they were at the forefront, praying and believing for miracles. This involvement underscores the revival's inclusivity, showing that God's power knows no age limit.

The chapter further delves into **Mass Healings and Spontaneous Miracles**, where the supernatural became an expected part of the congregation's life. These instances of divine intervention brought the community together, reinforcing a collective belief in the miraculous.

Beyond the physical healings, the revival also witnessed **Healing Beyond Physical Ailments**, encompassing emotional and spiritual restoration. This holistic approach to healing underscores God's concern for our entire being, aiming to heal not just our bodies but also our hearts and spirits.

One of the most awe-inspiring aspects of the revival was the **Shekinah Glory**. Participants described experiencing a tangible presence of God, a visible manifestation of divine glory that filled the room and touched everyone present.

The **Notable Miracles** section recounts events that defy human logic, such as limbs being restored and incurable diseases disappearing instantly. These stories serve as powerful testimonials to God's unlimited power and serve as a beacon of hope, demonstrating that nothing is beyond His healing touch.

The legacy of Azusa Street, encapsulated in the **Legacy of Healing and Empowerment**, goes beyond the miracles themselves. It's about the faith that was ignited in the hearts of those who participated, a legacy that continues to inspire belief in God's miraculous power today.

Through these stories and reflections, my goal is to bridge the extraordinary events of the past with our current journey of faith. "Everyday Healings and Notable Miracles" reminds us of the endless possibilities when we believe in the power of God to intervene in our lives. This chapter is an invitation to deepen our faith, to live in expectation of God's mighty works in our own lives and in the world around us.

Reflective Questions

1. The Upper Room as a Place of Miracles: How does the concept of a dedicated space for seeking God, like the upper room, inspire you to create a personal space for prayer and meditation in your own life?
2. Everyday Faith in Action: Can you recall a time when your faith transformed an ordinary moment into an extraordinary experience? How did that change your perspective on the power of faith in daily life?
3. The Role of the Youth: Reflect on the impact that young people had during the Azusa Street Revival. How can you encourage or mentor a younger person in their faith journey?
4. Mass Healings and Spontaneous Miracles: Have you ever witnessed or experienced a moment of divine intervention? How did it affect your belief in the power of prayer?
5. Legacy of Healing and Empowerment: Considering the legacy of the Azusa Street

Revival, what legacy of faith do you hope to leave for future generations?

Actionable Steps

- **Cultivate a Heart of Expectancy**: Just as the congregants of the Azusa Street Revival expected miracles, approach your prayer life with the expectancy of God's intervention.
- **Equip Yourself with Knowledge of the Word**: Immerse yourself in scripture to strengthen your faith and understanding of God's promises of healing and restoration.
- **Engage in Acts of Faith**: Take practical steps to exercise your faith through prayer, fasting, and laying on of hands, remembering that faith without works is dead.

Journaling Prompt

Reflect on a situation in your life that needs a touch from God. Imagine yourself in the upper room at Azusa Street, laying your need before Him in faith. Write a prayer expressing your desire for His

EVERYDAY HEALINGS AND NOTABLE MIRACLES

CHAPTER II
BROTHER SEYMOUR

In your walk with God, remember, it's not the grandeur of your actions that speaks loudest but the depth of your humility and the sincerity of your love. Just as Brother Seymour showed us, it is through our "conscious weakness and lowliness before God" that His power flows most freely through us. Let this be the cornerstone of your faith and service.

"But he gives more grace. Therefore, it says, 'God opposes the proud but gives grace to the humble.'" - James 4:6 (NKJV)

Chapter 11 brings to life the story of a pivotal figure, **Brother Seymour**, whose humility and spiritual depth became the cornerstone of one of the most transformative movements in recent history. His voice, rich and resonating, wasn't just heard; it was felt. It carried a divine authority that drew people not to him but through him, to a deeper communion with God. Seymour wasn't merely a preacher; he was a conduit for Christ's love, making every word, every message, not just heard, but deeply felt by those who listened.

Seymour's vision for the church was groundbreaking. He dreamed of a community where everyone was welcome, breaking down the walls that divided people by race or background. This dream became a reality at Azusa Street, shining as a beacon of hope and a blueprint for what the church could be. His commitment to **ecumenism** underscored a belief that the body of Christ was meant to transcend all man-made boundaries, reflecting the unity for which Jesus prayed.

In his teachings, Seymour underscored **salvation and sanctification** as the bedrock of a believer's life, treating the baptism in the Holy Spirit as an empowerment for service rather than a spiritual badge of honor. He championed **speaking in tongues** as a biblical sign, yet he firmly believed the genuine mark of Spirit baptism was a life overflowing with God's love. This perspective shifted the focus from seeking spectacular spiritual manifestations to cultivating the fruit of the Spirit in one's life.

Seymour's wisdom in maintaining **order in services** reflected his acute attunement to the Holy Spirit's movement. He knew when to allow the free expression of spiritual gifts and when to gently guide the congregation back to a place of listening and reverence, always with a gentle touch or a word that brought correction without condemnation.

The enduring message of Seymour's life is a call to the core values of the Gospel: love, humility, and unity. His journey reminds us that true spiritual movements are not born out of grand displays but through the faithful, heart-deep prayers of those fully surrendered to God. Inspired by Seymour's life, let's pursue a deeper filling of the Spirit, seeking not our glory but the expansion of God's kingdom on earth. His legacy challenges us to look beyond our desires for spiritual experiences to the more profound call of living out the love and unity that the Spirit so powerfully works within us.

Reflective Questions

1. How can we cultivate humility in our spiritual walk, following the example of Brother Seymour?
2. In what ways can we contribute to breaking down barriers that divide people within our communities and churches?
3. Reflect on the importance of salvation and sanctification in your life. How do these foundations shape your relationship with God?
4. How do you balance the desire for spiritual gifts with the pursuit of a life characterized by the fruits of the Spirit?
5. Considering Seymour's legacy, what steps can you take to foster unity and love in your surroundings?

Actionable Steps

- **Cultivate a deep personal relationship with God**, prioritizing time in prayer and meditation on His Word, allowing His Spirit to fill you with humility and love.

- **Equip yourself and others by sharing the message of love and unity** that Seymour championed, through small group discussions or community service.
- **Engage in acts of kindness and service**, demonstrating God's love in practical ways to those within and outside your church community.

Journaling Prompt

Reflect on the moments in your life where you've felt most connected to God's purpose for you. How can you embody the humility and love that Brother Seymour lived by, in your daily actions and interactions with others? Consider the barriers within your own heart that might need breaking down to fully embrace God's vision of unity and love.

BROTHER SEYMOUR

CHAPTER 12
THE DECLINE, SECOND SHOWER, AND DEMISE

In every journey, there are times of both sunshine and rain. It's in these moments that our faith is both tested and strengthened. As we've seen in this chapter, the story of the Azusa Street Revival is no exception. It was a time of tremendous growth and spiritual awakening, but not without its challenges and moments of decline.

"Be strong and of good courage; do not be afraid, nor be dismayed, for the Lord your God is with you wherever you go." - Joshua 1:9 (NKJV)

In this chapter, we continue the story of the Azusa Street Revival, focusing on its later stages. This period is marked by both progress and challenges. I want to take you through these significant moments, reflecting on what they taught us and how they shaped our journey.

The revival took a big step by **purchasing the mission building for $15,000**. This move was about more than just buying property; it was about creating a stable place for our growing community. It showed our commitment to a long-term home for the spirit of revival to dwell.

However, this period wasn't without its difficulties. An early challenge was the **demand for financial accountability by Professor Carpenter**. This issue brought to light the need for openness in our financial dealings, reminding us of the importance of trust and integrity in all we do.

Another significant change was the introduction of **offering collections**. This shift sparked discussions within our community about maintaining our core values amidst practical needs. It was a moment of reflection on how we balance our spiritual principles with the realities of running a growing community.

Despite these challenges, **reports continued to affirm the spiritual vitality of the revival**. Lives were still being transformed, which was a testament to the unending power of faith and the Holy Spirit's work among us.

Yet, we faced doctrinal conflicts, especially regarding

stances on divorce and remarriage. These discussions tested our unity and commitment to holiness, highlighting the need for a compassionate and clear understanding of scripture.

The departure of key figures, like **Lucy Farrow, and the loss of our publication**, represented significant setbacks. These events underscored the complexity of leading a diverse movement, stressing the importance of shared vision and communication.

Despite these trials, the spirit of the revival endured. **The continuous transformations and healings** reminded us of the revival's foundational strength and the Holy Spirit's persistent work in our lives.

However, **the decline of the revival** began to show, with decreased attendance and a dilution of the original spirit that had fueled its success. This prompted reflections on what had made the revival thrive initially and what contributed to its gradual decline.

Internal conflicts over doctrine and leadership further complicated matters, straining relationships within our community and challenging us to revisit our foundational beliefs and practices.

Ultimately, **the loss of our publication** and **failed recovery attempts** marked a significant turning point. These challenges highlighted the importance of stewardship, unity, and perseverance. They reminded us that the essence of revival lies in the transformation of hearts and lives through the Holy Spirit's power.

As we reflect on this chapter, it's clear that the story of the Azusa Street Revival is about faith, resilience, and the relentless pursuit of God's presence. It reminds us that true revival is measured not by numbers or achievements but by the depth of our relationship with God and the impact of His love on the world around us.

Reflective Questions

1. How do the challenges faced during the later stages of the Azusa Street Revival mirror challenges in our own spiritual journeys today?
2. In what ways can we apply the lessons of perseverance and faith from this chapter to overcome obstacles in our lives and communities?
3. Reflect on the significance of unity and how it was both a strength and a challenge during the revival. How can we foster unity in our own contexts?
4. Consider the impact of leadership decisions during the decline of the revival. What can we

learn about the role of leadership in sustaining spiritual movements?
5. The revival's emphasis on the Holy Spirit's transformative power remains a powerful lesson. How can we seek and welcome this transformation in our lives today?

Actionable Steps

Cultivate a heart of resilience by regularly reflecting on Scripture and stories of faith that remind us of God's faithfulness through challenges.

Equip yourself with a deep understanding of God's Word to navigate doctrinal differences with grace and wisdom.

Engage in community building, emphasizing unity and love, drawing lessons from the revival's early days of harmony and collective worship.

Journaling **Prompt**

Reflect on a moment in your life when you experienced a personal 'revival' or a deepening of your faith. What lessons did you learn during that time, and how have those lessons shaped your journey with God since then?

THE DECLINE, SECOND SHOWER, AND DEMISE

KEYS TO EXPERIENCING AZUSA FIRE OFFICIAL WORKBOOK

CHAPTER 13
THE AZUSA STREET LEGACY

Keep the faith and let your light shine. In every situation, God's grace is sufficient for you, and His power is made perfect in weakness.

2 Corinthians 12:9 (NKJV) - "And He said to me, 'My grace is sufficient for you, for My strength is made perfect in weakness.' Therefore most gladly I will rather boast in my infirmities, that the power of Christ may rest upon me."

In the latter years of the Azusa Street Mission, we saw a significant shift. The mission had to navigate through rough waters, especially as racial tensions began to surface. This was a tough period, and it led to a crucial decision: **to amend the mission's articles of incorporation**, specifying that its leadership would be people of color. This decision was not about exclusion but about creating a space where everyone could feel valued and heard, amidst an increasingly divisive atmosphere.

During **these years**, I remained steadfast in my commitment to the mission, despite dwindling numbers and support. It was a challenging time, but my focus never wavered from the vision that had ignited the revival in the first place. It's a testament to the fact that the true strength of a movement isn't just in its numbers but in the depth of its conviction.

The loss of **William Seymour** in 1922 was a pivotal moment for the mission and for me. It marked the end of an era, but also the beginning of a legacy that would continue to inspire and challenge future generations. Even in his absence, the principles of love, unity, and spiritual fervor that he championed remained a beacon of hope.

The years following my departure were tumultuous,

with legal battles and leadership struggles testing the resilience of the mission. Yet, despite these challenges, the spirit of Azusa Street lived on, through memorials, commemorations, and the countless lives transformed by the message of Pentecost.

One of the most remarkable aspects of the Azusa Street legacy is how it has been **memorialized** and celebrated over the years. From educational institutions to religious organizations, the revival's impact has been acknowledged and honored, underscoring its lasting influence on Christian faith and practice globally.

Indeed, the **enduring legacy** of Azusa Street speaks volumes about the power of the Holy Spirit to break down barriers and foster transformative change. It's a legacy that continues to empower and challenge us, urging us to seek greater unity, deeper love, and a more dynamic experience of the Spirit's work in our lives.

Looking to the future, the prophetic vision for **new movements of the Spirit** invites us to stay open and expectant. The journey of faith is ever-evolving, filled with both victories and valleys. But it's in this journey that we find the true essence of revival - a continuous, Spirit-led transformation that transcends time and circumstance.

As we reflect on the story of Azusa Street, let's carry forward its torch with courage and faith, ever mindful of the Spirit's power to renew and unite. Let's embrace the legacy of unity, love, and revival, and may we always be ready for the more that God has in store.

Reflective Questions

1. How does the legacy of Azusa Street inspire you in your faith journey today?
2. In what ways can we embody the principles of love and unity in our communities?
3. What role does the Holy Spirit play in your personal spiritual experience?
4. How can we remain open and expectant for new movements of the Spirit in our time?
5. What steps can you take to foster a deeper sense of community among believers from diverse backgrounds?

Actionable Steps

- **Cultivate** a heart of humility and openness to the Spirit's leading in your life.
- **Equip** yourself and others with the knowledge of God's Word and the history of the Spirit's movements.

- **Engage** in acts of love and service that build bridges and foster unity within the body of Christ.

Journaling Prompt

Reflect on the impact of the Azusa Street revival on modern Christianity. Consider how you can incorporate its principles of faith, unity, and the power of the Holy Spirit into your daily life and community.

KEYS TO EXPERIENCING AZUSA FIRE OFFICIAL WORKBOOK

CHAPTER 14
THE PILGRIMS OF AZUSA STREET

Let's take courage in the fact that every small step we take in faith has the potential to leave a lasting impact, much like the pilgrims of Azusa Street. Their journey reminds us that faithfulness in our walk with God can ripple through time and across continents, inspiring countless others.

"Therefore, my beloved brethren, be steadfast, immovable, always abounding in the work of the Lord, knowing that your labor is not in vain in the Lord." - 1 Corinthians 15:58 (NKJV)

In Chapter 14, "The Pilgrims of Azusa Street," we dive into the stories of those brave souls who carried the fire of the Azusa Street Revival far and wide. These folks, affectionately known as "the pilgrims of Los Angeles," played a crucial role in spreading Pentecostalism across the globe.

The journey of spreading **Azusa's influence** was nothing short of extraordinary. As these pilgrims ventured into new territories—whether it was bustling cities like Oakland and Chicago or serene places like Portland, or even the southern charm of states like North Carolina and Alabama—they planted seeds of Pentecostal faith. Their stories paint a vivid picture of Azusa Street's deep and lasting impact.

Among these trailblazers, **G.B. Cashwell** stands out. His revivals in the South laid a foundation for Pentecostalism there. Likewise, **C.H. Mason** took the message back to Tennessee and the Deep South, enriching the spiritual landscape with teachings on sanctification and the baptism in the Holy Spirit.

Glenn Cook's travels from Lamont, Oklahoma, to Chicago and Indianapolis showcased the unity and shared mission of Azusa Street revivalists. They were all driven by a desire to share their newfound faith.

The involvement of **children in the revival** is a heartwarming testament to the Holy Spirit's power. Their divine wisdom and participation added an innocence to the revival that underscored its message: the Kingdom of God belongs to such as these.

The birth of **Oneness Pentecostalism** reveals the diversity within the Pentecostal movement. This development highlights the evolving nature of Pentecostal theology.

The **missionary work** of people like Lucy Farrow and Owen "Irish" Lee showed Azusa Street's global reach. Their journeys to Liberia and Ireland, respectively, underlined the universal appeal of the revival's message.

Children's roles in the revival were unforgettable. Speaking in tongues and delivering divine messages, they showed the transformative power of the Holy Spirit—age was no barrier.

As **new denominations emerged**, including the Assemblies of God and the United Pentecostal Church International, we see institutions that have significantly shaped global Christianity.

Through it all, **Seymour's legacy** remained a source of inspiration. His leadership and commitment to the Holy Spirit's guidance continued to influence long after the revival's initial days.

Lastly, the **enduring spirit of Azusa Street** invites us to reflect on our faith journey. It challenges us to embrace unity, love, and spiritual fervor, encouraging us to carry the torch of revival in our lives and communities, igniting the world with the fire of Pentecostal faith.

Reflective Questions

1. How can we cultivate a faith that's open to the leading of the Holy Spirit, as demonstrated by the early Pentecostals?
2. What lessons can we learn from the challenges and successes of spreading the Pentecostal message?
3. In what ways does the journey of the Azusa Street pilgrims inspire you to share your faith with others?
4. Consider the role of unity and diversity in the early Pentecostal movement. How can these principles be applied in today's faith communities?
5. Reflect on the lasting impact of the Azusa Street revival. What does this teach us about the significance of our own spiritual contributions?

Actionable Steps

- **Cultivate** an environment in your community or church that welcomes the Holy Spirit's movement and guidance.
- **Equip** yourself and others with knowledge of the Pentecostal heritage and the foundational beliefs that sparked a global movement.
- **Engage** in personal and communal prayer, seeking a fresh outpouring of the Holy Spirit in your life and the lives of those around you.

Journaling **Prompt**

REFLECT on the influence of the Azusa Street revival in shaping modern Christianity. How does understanding this heritage inspire you to live out your faith boldly and share the message of the Holy Spirit with others.

CHAPTER 15
BEGINNING OF A WORLDWIDE REVIVAL

Let's hold onto the truth that the Spirit of God, which ignited a global movement from a humble street in Los Angeles, is the same Spirit that moves in and through us today. This same Spirit empowers, guides, and propels us forward, encouraging us to spread the light of Christ to the ends of the earth.

Acts 1:8 (NKJV) - "But you shall receive power when the Holy Spirit has come upon you; and you shall be witnesses to Me in Jerusalem, and in all Judea and Samaria, and to the end of the earth."

This revival, starting from **Azusa Street**, spread like wildfire across the globe. Imagine a tiny spark in Los Angeles igniting a passion that reached every corner of the world, uniting people from different cultures and walks of life in a profound spiritual experience. This revival didn't know any limits; it leaped across oceans, touching hearts far and wide.

At the heart of this global spread was a simple newsletter called **"The Apostolic Faith."** This wasn't just a publication; it was a beacon of hope. It shared stories of people's lives being transformed through faith, proving that words, when touched by the Holy Spirit, have the power to reach and change lives, no matter the distance.

The journey began with the **First Apostolic Faith Missionaries**, brave souls like Andrew G. Johnson and Alfred and Lillian Garr, who felt called to share this revival with the world. They set out with little more than faith and a suitcase, teaching us that answering God's call is the first step toward witnessing His miraculous works.

Then, there were the **Veteran Missionaries' Second Calling**. These were individuals who, after serving on mission fields, came to Azusa Street, received new power, and went back with a fresh anointing. Their stories remind us that God always has more for us, a deeper relationship and a new chapter in serving His kingdom.

Of course, the journey wasn't without its **Challenges**. Early missionaries learned that speaking in tongues wasn't a universal key to language barriers. This lesson taught them and teaches us about the need for cultural sensitivity, perseverance, love, and the realization that mission work requires more than just spiritual gifts.

The **Global Impact through Publications** demonstrated how the spread of Pentecostalism wasn't confined to physical travels. The written word, anointed by the Holy Spirit, planted seeds in nations worldwide, blooming into diverse, vibrant expressions of faith.

Hearty Send-Offs and Commitment at Azusa Street were special. The community's practice of supporting missionaries with prayer, song, and resources illustrates a collective commitment to sharing the gospel, showing us today how to support those called to spread the word.

T.B. Barratt and the European Revival is a powerful example of how one person's encounter with the Holy Spirit can impact a continent. Barratt's ministry in Europe seeded a spiritual harvest that continues to grow, showing the incredible effect of shared faith and testimony.

The story in **South Africa** is a beautiful illustration of the revival's power to cross racial and linguistic divides.

The ministry of John G. Lake among diverse communities laid the groundwork for some of the largest Pentecostal churches today, showcasing the Holy Spirit's uniting power.

Lastly, the **Legacy and Expansion** of the Azusa Street revival teaches us that what began in a humble mission has grown into a worldwide movement. This legacy is measured not just in numbers but in transformed lives through the Holy Spirit's power—a legacy we're invited to continue.

As you ponder this journey from Azusa Street to the ends of the earth, remember that the same Spirit active then is still moving today, calling us to carry the flame of revival wherever we may go.

Reflective Questions

1. How does the Azusa Street revival's impact on global Christianity inspire your own faith journey?
2. Reflect on the role of "The Apostolic Faith" publication in spreading the revival. How does this highlight the power of sharing testimonies?

3. Consider the challenges faced by early missionaries. What lessons can we learn about perseverance and faith in the face of adversity?
4. T.B. Barratt brought revival to Europe after his encounter with the Holy Spirit. How can one person's transformed life impact many?
5. The legacy of Azusa Street continues today. In what ways can we contribute to this ongoing movement of the Holy Spirit?

Actionable Steps

- **Cultivate** a heart for global missions by regularly praying for countries and people groups across the world. Start with one country each week, learning about its culture and specific challenges, and dedicate time to pray for the believers and missionaries there.
- **Equip** yourself with knowledge about the history of global Christianity and current missions efforts. Read books, watch documentaries, and follow organizations engaged in missions work to understand the needs and how the gospel is advancing today.

- **Engage** in practical support for missions by either volunteering for short-term missions trips, supporting missionaries financially, or getting involved in local outreach programs that have a global impact. Your contribution, no matter how small, plays a part in the great commission.

Journaling Prompt

Reflect on the story of the Azusa Street revival spreading across the globe. Consider the courage, faith, and dedication of those early missionaries. In your journal, answer the question: "How can I embody the spirit of an Azusa Street missionary in my everyday life?" Think about the ways you can share the gospel in your community, support global missions, or even simply pray for a revival in your own heart and around the world.

BEGINNING OF A WORLDWIDE REVIVAL

CHAPTER 16
UNLOCKING AZUSA FIRE

God is always on the move, seeking those whose hearts are fully His to manifest His glory and power. As you open your heart to Him, expect to see His kingdom come in your life in ways beyond what you can ask or imagine.

"For God has not given us a spirit of fear, but of power and of love and of a sound mind." - 2 Timothy 1:7 NKJV

Let's embark on a journey back to **1906**, to a humble mission on Azusa Street in Los Angeles. This wasn't just any event; it was a divine explosion that marked the beginning of a spiritual awakening impacting the globe. **The Azusa Street Revival** stands as a monumental chapter in the history of Christianity, showcasing the power of God moving among His people. This revival didn't just happen; it was birthed from a deep, collective hunger for more of God, a desire that transcended race, culture, and social status.

At the heart of this movement was a simple yet profound truth: God's presence can transform the ordinary into the extraordinary. As believers gathered in that modest mission, the Holy Spirit moved powerfully, bringing about miraculous healings, speaking in tongues, and prophecies. These were not just for show but were signs of God's kingdom breaking into the world in tangible ways. **The miracles** that occurred were a testament to God's love and power, reminding us that when we seek Him wholeheartedly, the impossible becomes possible.

Unity in diversity was perhaps one of Azusa's most striking aspects. In an era marked by segregation and division, the revival stood as a beacon of God's inclusive love. **The gathering of diverse believers** under one roof, seeking God's face together, was a powerful demonstration of the kingdom of Heaven on earth. This unity wasn't superficial; it was a divine knitting together of hearts and spirits, showcasing the beauty of God's family in its multifaceted diversity.

Leadership during this revival was unlike any seen before. It wasn't about titles or hierarchy but about humility and sensitivity to the Holy Spirit's leading. **William Seymour**, a man marked by his deep love for God and his humble heart, led not from a position of power but from a posture of submission to God's will. This approach to leadership, centered on following the Holy Spirit's guidance, was crucial for sustaining the revival's momentum and impact.

Yet, at the core of the Azusa Street Revival, and what should be at the core of our lives, is the pursuit of God Himself. It's a stark reminder that our primary call is to seek God above all else. **The hunger for God's presence** was the fuel that kept the revival burning. It wasn't about chasing after signs and wonders but about a deep, insatiable desire to know God more intimately and to experience His presence more fully.

As we look to the future, believing for another great move of God, Azusa Street offers both inspiration and instruction. We're reminded that **revival starts with a hunger for God** that refuses to be satisfied with the status quo. It requires **unity among believers**, transcending our differences to seek God's face together. It calls for **leadership that is humble, willing to follow**

where the Spirit leads, and it focuses us on the ultimate goal: seeking God, not just His handiwork.

Azusa Street wasn't just a historical event; it's a blueprint for us today, showing us that when we come together in humility, unity, and desperate hunger for God, He moves in ways beyond what we could ask or imagine. **The Azusa Street Revival** invites us to dare to dream of what God can do through us when we lay aside our agendas and simply seek Him with all our hearts. It challenges us to prepare for what's ahead, to be ready to ride the waves of His Spirit, and to play our part in the greatest move of God the world has yet to see.

Reflective Questions

1. How can we cultivate a deeper hunger for God's presence in our personal lives and our communities?
2. In what ways can we foster unity within our diverse body of believers, reflecting the unity seen during the Azusa Street Revival?
3. What does true spiritual leadership look like in the context of a move of God, and how can we embody these qualities?

4. How can we prioritize seeking God Himself over the signs and wonders that may accompany His presence?
5. As we look forward to a potential greater move of God, how can we prepare our hearts and communities to be receptive and responsive to the Holy Spirit?

Actionable Steps

- **Cultivate** a daily practice of seeking God's presence through prayer, worship, and reading His Word, inviting the Holy Spirit to guide and direct our lives.
- **Equip** ourselves and our communities with knowledge and understanding of past revivals, especially the Azusa Street Revival, to learn from both their successes and their challenges.
- **Engage** in intentional community-building efforts that embrace diversity and foster unity among believers, mirroring the inclusivity of the Azusa Street Revival.

Journaling Prompt

Reflect on your personal desire for God's presence. How does the story of the Azusa Street Revival inspire you to pursue a deeper relationship with God? What practical steps can you take to cultivate a revival-like atmosphere in your own life and community?

UNLOCKING AZUSA FIRE

KEYS TO EXPERIENCING AZUSA FIRE OFFICIAL WORKBOOK

FAITH AND FLAME PRESS
IGNITING THE FLAMES OF FAITH

Faith and Flame Press is a Christian book publishing company that is passionate about igniting the flames of faith in the hearts of readers around the world. Our mission is to publish books that inspire, enlighten, and uplift the spirit, and help readers deepen their understanding of their faith and spirituality.

At Faith and Flame Press, we believe that books have the power to transform lives and to shape the world we live in. That's why we are committed to publishing books that are not only spiritually uplifting but also intellectually stimulating, well-researched, and thought-provoking.

www.ingramcontent.com/pod-product-compliance
Lightning Source LLC
Chambersburg PA
CBHW070123100426
42744CB00010B/1904